Exploding Stars

Illustrations: Janet Moneymaker
Design/Editing: Marjie Bassler

Copyright © 2023 by Rebecca Woodbury, Ph.D.

All rights reserved. No part of this publication may be reproduced, stored in a retrieval system, or transmitted, in any form or by any means, electronic, mechanical, photocopying, recording, or otherwise, without prior written permission from the publisher. No part of this book may be reproduced in any manner whatsoever without written permission.

Exploding Stars
ISBN 978-1-950415-47-2

Published by Gravitas Publications Inc.
Imprint: Real Science-4-Kids
www.gravitaspublications.com
www.realscience4kids.com

RS4K

Photo credits:
Cover—ESA & Garrelt Mellema (Leiden University, the Netherlands);
1. Hubble/NASA, ESA, F. Paresce (INAF-IASF, Italy), the WFC3 Science Oversight Committee;
2. Hubble/NASA, ESA, C.R. O'Dell (Vanderbilt University), The Hubble Heritage Team (STScI/AURA);
3. ESA & Garrelt Mellema (Leiden University, the Netherlands)

Have you ever looked at the stars at night and wondered what they are made of and whether they last forever?

"Do you think stars are born and die?"

"Maybe."

A **star** is an object in space that is made of **hydrogen** and **helium atoms.** It makes its own **light energy and heat energy** when hydrogen atoms combine to make helium.

REVIEW
ATOMS

Atoms are tiny building blocks that can link together.

Atoms make up everything we touch, taste, smell, and see.

Matter is the name for everything we touch, taste, smell, and see.

Stars are born inside a huge cloud of gas and dust.

The blue dots are young, very hot stars.

1

A star dies when it runs out of the hydrogen it uses for fuel.

I use cheese for fuel.

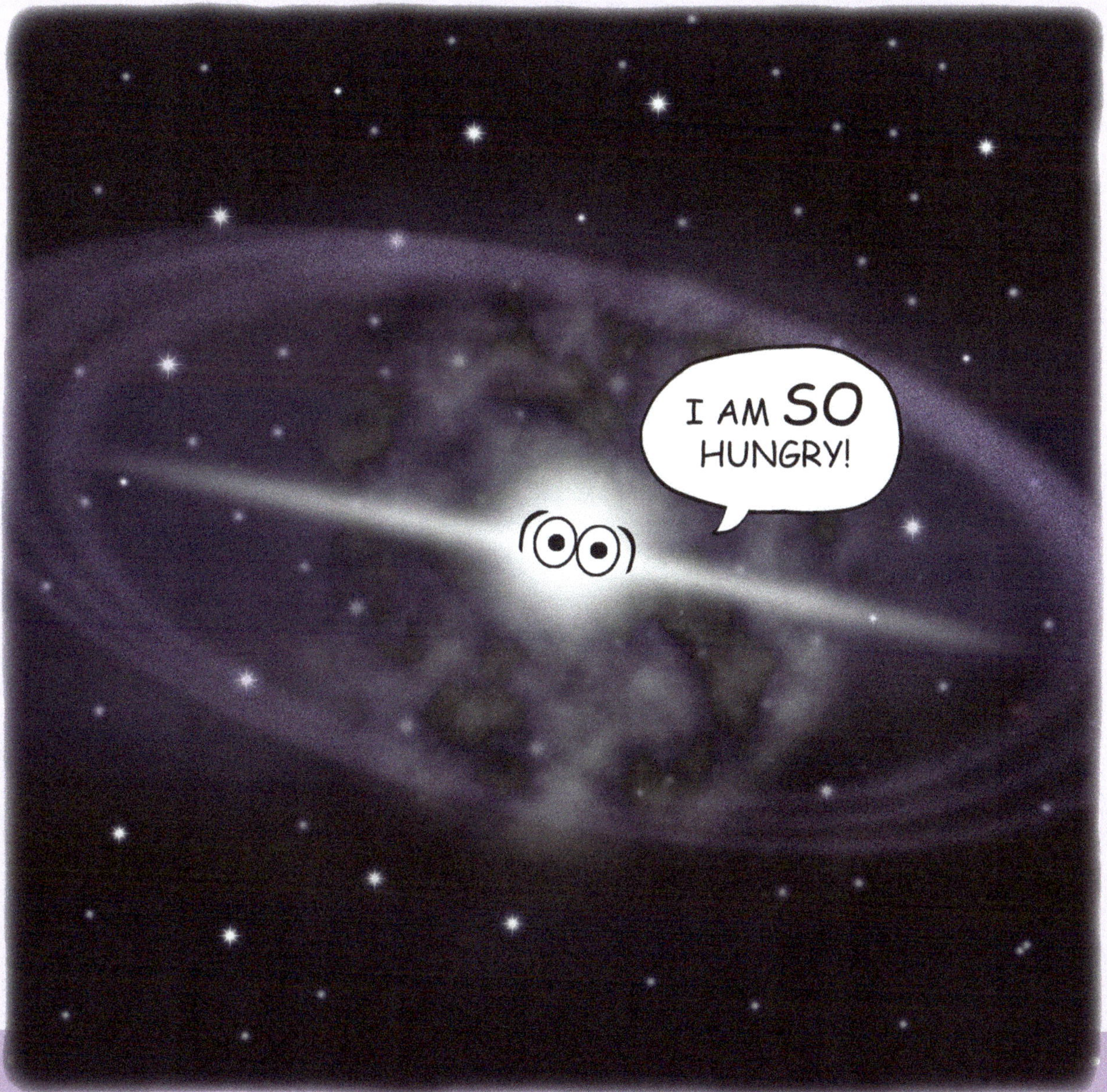
I AM SO HUNGRY!

A big star that runs out of fuel ends its life in a huge explosion called a **supernova.** A supernova is extremely bright, but its light fades quickly.

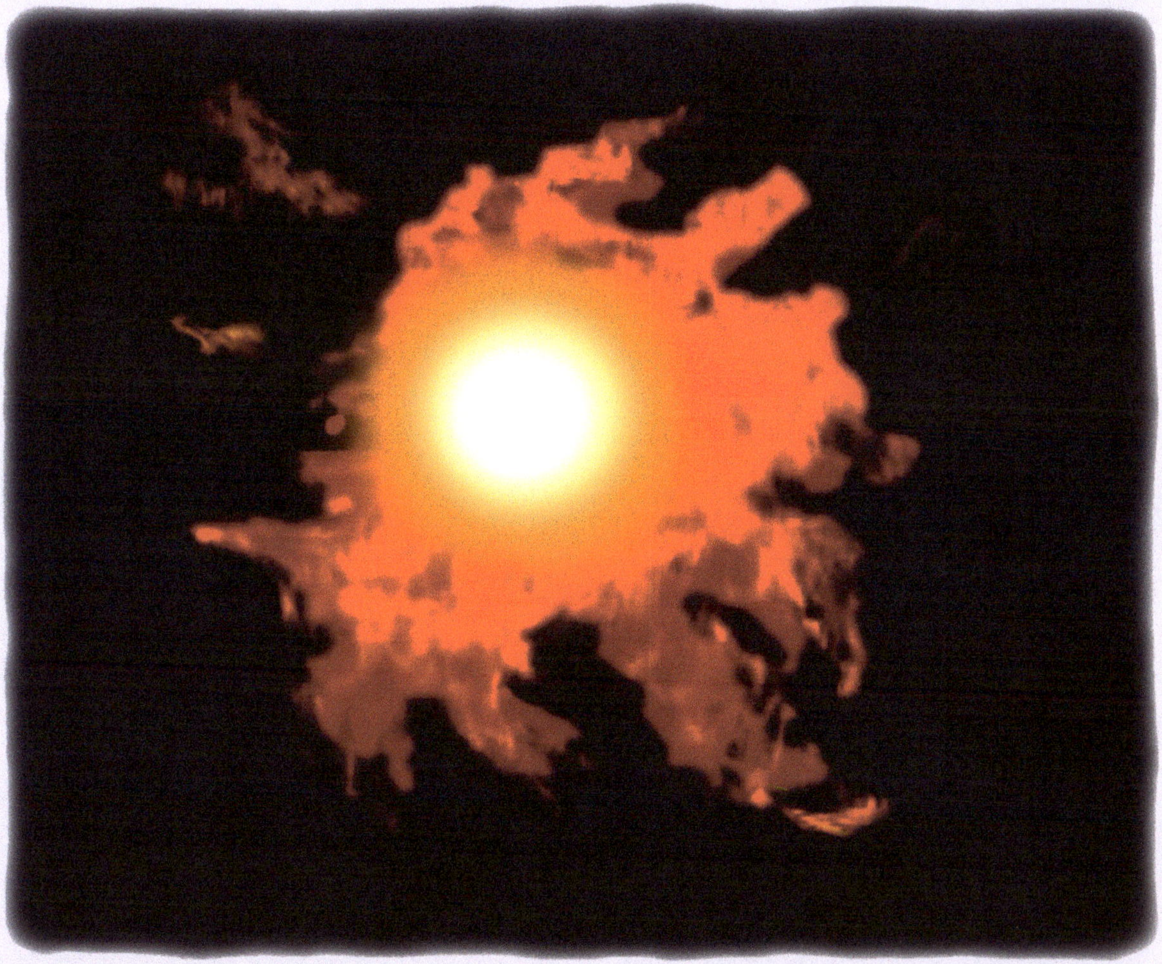

After a star explodes in a supernova, it leaves behind a cloud of gas and dust called a **nebula.**

Nebulas are beautiful.

Yes. And they are all different.

2

A supernova can also leave behind a **white dwarf star** or a **black hole**.

Black Hole

A supernova explosion blasts the dying star's matter into space.

3

Many different kinds of atoms are scattered into the universe by a supernova, including hydrogen, helium, carbon, and even gold.

Wow! Look at those atoms fly!

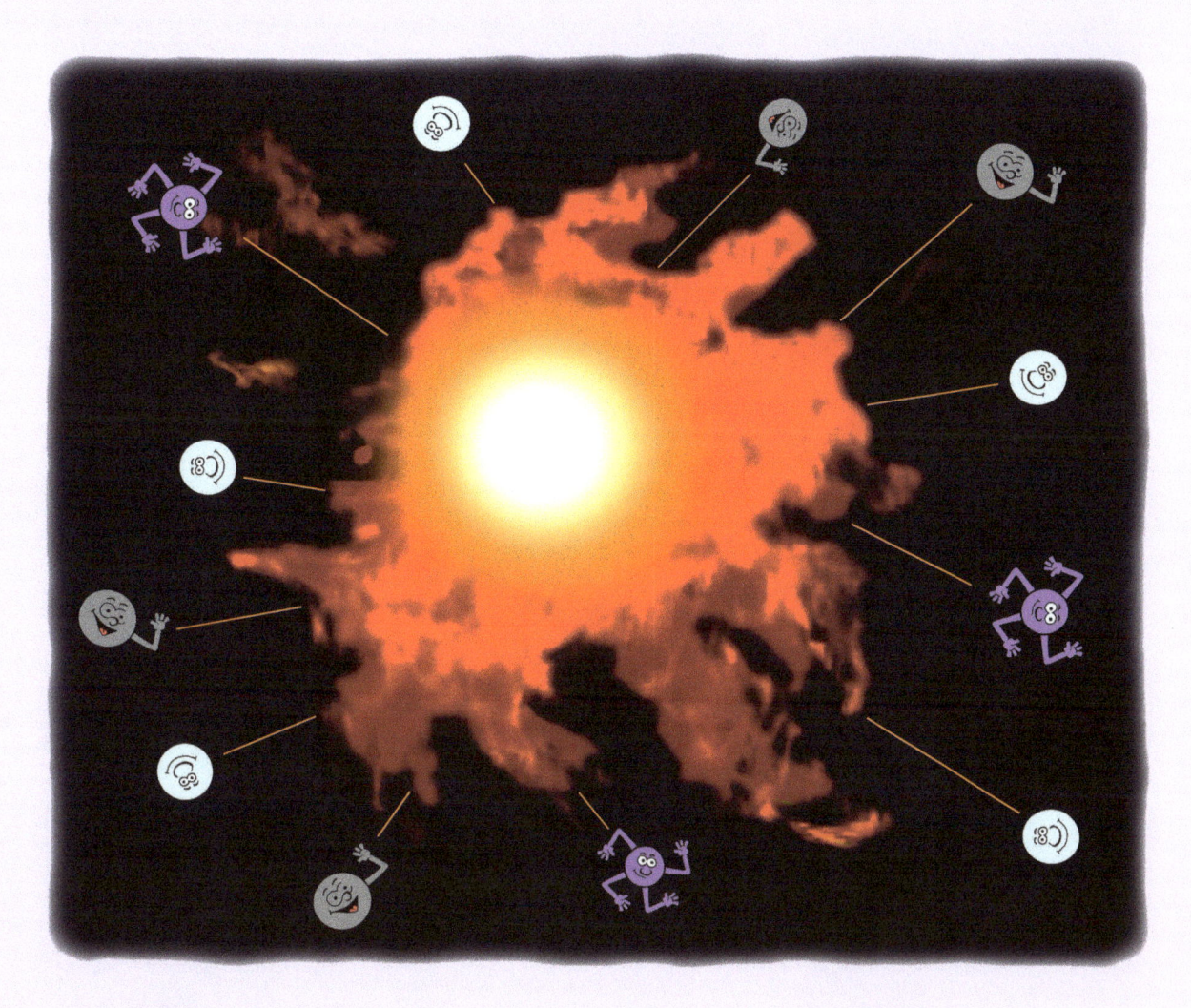

hydrogen atom   helium atom   carbon atom

All the atoms that make up everything on Earth were once part of stars. You are made from stars too!

Me too!

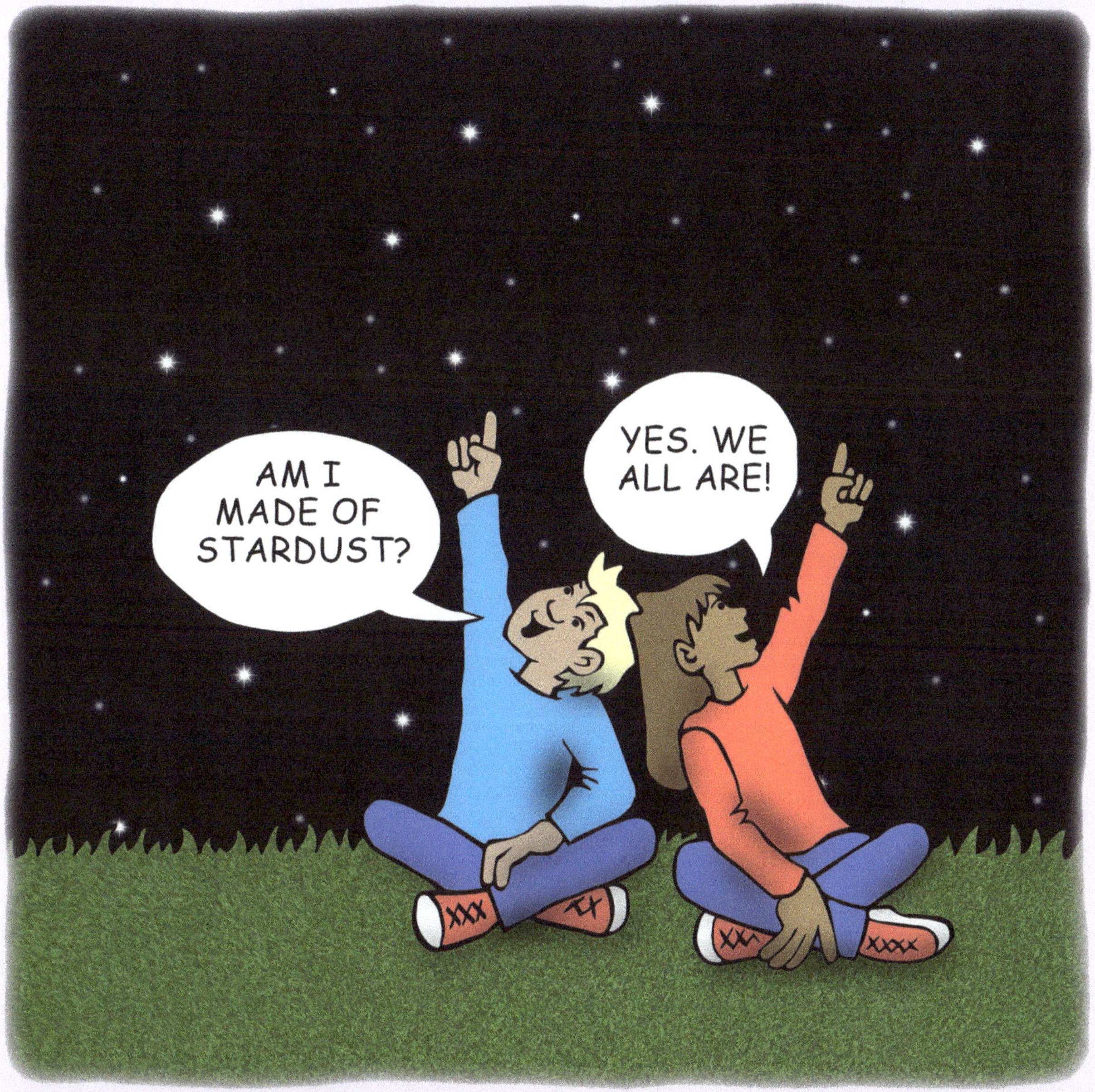
AM I MADE OF STARDUST?
YES. WE ALL ARE!

How to say science words

atom (AA-tuhm)

carbon (KAHR-buhn)

heat energy (HEET EN-uhr-jee)

helium (HEE-lee-uhm)

hydrogen (HIY-druh-juhn)

light energy (LIYT EN-uhr-jee)

matter (MAA-tuhr)

nebula (NE-byuh-luh)

science (SIY-uhns)

supernova (soo-puhr-NOH-vuh)

What questions do you have about EXPLODING STARS?

Learn More Real Science!

Complete science curricula from Real Science-4-Kids

Focus On Series

Unit study for elementary and middle school levels

Chemistry
Biology
Physics
Geology
Astronomy

Exploring Science Series

Graded series for levels K–8. Each book contains 4 chapters of:

Chemistry
Biology
Physics
Geology
Astronomy

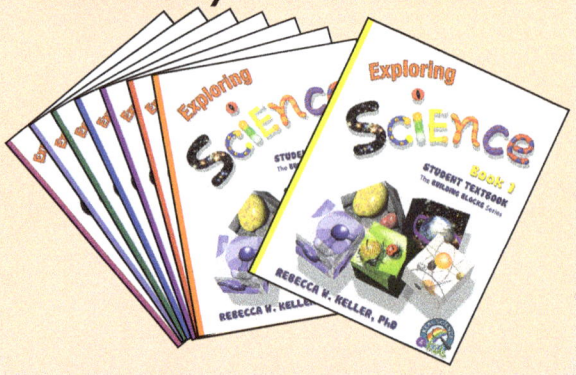

CPSIA information can be obtained
at www.ICGtesting.com
Printed in the USA
BVHW011233170223
658735BV00012B/1098